GREAT EXIT PROJECTS ON THE COLUMBIAN EXCHANGE

GREAT SOCIAL STUDIES EXIT PROJECTS™

GREAT EXIT PROJECTS ON THE COLUMBIAN EXCHANGE

Alana Benson

rosen publishing's rosen central®

New York

Published in 2020 by The Rosen Publishing Group, Inc.
29 East 21st Street, New York, NY 10010

First Edition

Library of Congress Cataloging-in-Publication Data

Names: Benson, Alana, author.
Title: Great exit projects on the Columbian Exchange / Alana Benson.
Description: First edition. | New York : Rosen Publishing, 2020. | Series: Great social studies exit projects | Includes bibliographical references and index.
Identifiers: LCCN 2018009231| ISBN 9781499440379 (library bound) | ISBN 9781499440362 (pbk.)
Subjects: LCSH: Columbus, Christopher—Juvenile literature. | Indians—First contact with Europeans—Juvenile literature. | America—Discovery and exploration—Spanish—Juvenile literature.
Classification: LCC E111 .B478 2019 | DDC 970.01/6—dc23
LC record available at https://lccn.loc.gov/2018009231

Manufactured in the United States of America

CONTENTS

6 INTRODUCTION

9 CHAPTER ONE
MORE THAN JUST SMALLPOX

17 CHAPTER TWO
THE ORIGINS OF PIZZA

27 CHAPTER THREE
HORSES, LLAMAS, AND OXEN, OH MY!

35 CHAPTER FOUR
CONQUERORS AND THE CONQUERED

43 CHAPTER FIVE
THE GOOD, THE BAD, AND THE UGLY OF THE COLUMBIAN EXCHANGE

52 GLOSSARY
54 FOR MORE INFORMATION
58 FOR FURTHER READING
59 BIBLIOGRAPHY
61 INDEX

INTRODUCTION

In 1492 Columbus sailed the ocean blue. So goes the rhyme for kids learning about world history. But is that really the whole story? Many people take the fact that "Columbus discovered America" at face value, but there is a lot more to the tale. First of all, it's hard to discover a land that already exists and supports large populations of people—namely, the Native Americans. And as far as Christopher Columbus being the first European to set foot on the American continent, that title had already been claimed, roughly 492 years earlier by Viking explorer Leif Erikson.

While it's possible other people came first (theories range from Irish monks to a Chinese fleet, though these have mostly been debunked), the first verifiable visit to the Americas by a European was Erikson, who was sent to Greenland to convert the settlers there to Christianity. As the story goes, he sailed off course and ended up in a place he called "Vinland," or "Wine Land," because of all the abundant grapes and timber. There are archaeological remains of this visit on the northern tip of Newfoundland, and even though Erikson was fond of this new wine-filled land, he didn't stay long. Erikson and his family had a run-in with the people already living there, during which they killed a group of Thule people, a Native American tribe that predated the Inuit. Understandably, the Thule did not take kindly to this.

Christopher Columbus, the second recorded European to sail to America, was born in 1451, in Italy, and worked as a trader for a time in Lisbon, where he learned to sail, navigate, and make maps. In 1492, Christopher Columbus did in fact sail the ocean

Christopher Columbus was actually the second European to "find" North America, after Leif Erikson stumbled across the continent almost five hundred years earlier.

blue, although he thought he was sailing through a different body of water. Columbus was unaware of the American continent, like almost all Europeans at that time. Common thought held that there were only the European, Asian, and African landmasses, and Columbus believed that he had arrived in Southeast Asia. Columbus's journey is celebrated with Columbus Day, a holiday many people view with despair because this journey contributed to the eventual decimation of many Native Americans and their cultures. While Columbus was not the first person to cross the Atlantic, it was his journey that kick-started the Columbian Exchange, or the trade of plants, animals, people, disease, and ideas across the Atlantic Ocean that permanently altered our world.

Project-based learning incorporates real-world strategies and encourages making connections across subjects and concepts. Exit projects are projects developed using the accumulation of a student's knowledge on a particular subject and can be used as part of project-based learning. These projects may include mapping, letter writing, and argumentative debate. They promote the use of primary sources and inspire students to ask their own questions and pose new theories. The projects provided in this book on the Columbian Exchange are by no means the limit of what students can do to show mastery over the topic. They are merely a jumping-off point and serve as models from which students can show their own skill and creativity.

CHAPTER ONE

MORE THAN JUST SMALLPOX

Christopher Columbus long wondered if he could reach China by sailing across the Atlantic Ocean. For many years, no one was interested in his proposed voyage—at least not until he convinced Queen Isabella and King Ferdinand of

The arrival of Europeans led to the large-scale devastation of many Native American tribes.

Spain to finance the trip. He sailed from August to October of 1492 with three ships, the *Niña*, the *Pinta*, and the *Santa Maria*. The first time they spotted land was an island in the Bahamas. Upon meeting the native people there, Columbus called them Indians—because he thought they were from India—since he thought he had sailed around the world. Little did he know that he was in fact on a completely different continent.

Columbus and his men sailed to a few other islands, gathered up some goodies to take home to the king and queen, and returned to Spain. When he presented his royal sponsors with turkeys, pineapples, and prisoners he had taken from the islands, they were so impressed with his findings that they were happy to fund other ventures. Columbus returned three more times, bringing horses and other animals, and even making it to the mainland. He died in 1506, still ignorant of the fact that he had not actually sailed to South Asia.

QUESTION 1 **THE EXPLORERS WHO CAME AFTER COLUMBUS FOUND MASSIVE EMPIRES, ESPECIALLY IN CENTRAL AND SOUTH AMERICA. HOW DID THE ARRIVAL OF THE EUROPEANS AFFECT THESE EMPIRES IN THE LONG TERM?**

If Columbus didn't even find America first, why is he such a big deal? It is less about Columbus and more about what Columbus's journey allowed to happen afterward. Without that journey, and the subsequent explorations by other Europeans, the colonization of the Americas would never have happened. Native groups in the Americas would live very different lives than they do today.

When talking about the Columbian Exchange, or any time period when Europeans ventured across the Atlantic to the Americas, the perspective is nearly always from the European side. It's the "Old World" and the "New World," but that's hardly comprehensive. When you embark on these projects, remember that many of the sources you might find are from the European perspective. One way of enhancing these projects is to use sources provided by native groups to understand their different viewpoints. Many traditional oral stories from these cultures have been written down and are available online.

DISEASES DOING THE DIRTY WORK

In the early 1500s, the Incan Empire was led by Huayna Capac. This ruler died of smallpox in roughly 1527—about five years before Francisco Pizarro, the man who would eventually be responsible for the takedown of the Incan Empire, even arrived. After Huayna died, his sons became entangled in a civil war. This civil war destroyed the Incan population, spread smallpox (blood and physical contact are great ways to spread disease), and crippled their economy. Atahuallpa, Huayna's younger son, emerged as the victor, but the empire he won was ravaged by war and disease, making the Inca a target. At this point, Francisco Pizarro, a Spanish conquistador, arranged a meeting with the Inca's new leader. The conquistador and his 180 men told Atahuallpa he could bring 3,000 unarmed men to the meeting. When Atahuallpa showed up, with no weapons, Pizarro open fire on the Inca soldiers, massacring them, and took Atahuallpa as prisoner. Pizarro ransomed Atahuallpa for gold and silver, and after his people delivered the goods, Pizarro killed Atahuallpa anyway.

PROJECT 1
CHRONICLING A PEOPLE

Using your knowledge of the arrival of the Europeans and the consequent effects on native groups, write a letter from one of the leaders of the South and Central American empires, like Atahuallpa of the Inca, or Montezuma II, the Aztec ruler eventually conquered by Hernán Cortés, to their future people. Use both your knowledge of the ancient cultures and some research on the descendants of these great rulers. Use the Internet History Sourcebooks Project provided online by Fordham University at https://sourcebooks.fordham.edu to find accounts in order to get an idea of what these encounters were like.

- Pick a ruler, particularly one who witnessed the arrival of the Europeans and fought against them. Research their life, how they died, and what the state of their empire was like at that point in history.
- Find information about what happened to their empire in the years following their death. How many people in the empire died? When did the empire go into decline, and how quickly did it do so?
- Using the information gathered from your research, draw a map showing your chosen empire before the arrival of Europeans and in the years after. You can color code the map to show periods of expansion and decline. Make sure you label your map with dates and show its location in modern-day nations.
- Write a letter from the perspective of your chosen leader. Include descriptions of your last days of life, how you died, and your hopes for the future of your people. Make

Primary sources are a great way to get into the minds of people from the past, and many of them are available at libraries or online.

sure your letter mimics what you know about the leader's personality; for example, were you a kind and benevolent ruler, or cruel?

- Do some research on the modern populations that inhabit what was once the empire of your leader. Incorporate into your letter the following questions: How have your descendants fared? What echoes from the overthrow of your empire do you see in the modern population? Ask questions like, "What language do they speak?" and "What religion do they practice?" to get a better understanding of this. Also explore what country or countries your empire was incorporated into. Does it cross the boundaries of multiple nations? How has the land they inhabited changed since the fall of the empire?

- Present your map and your letter to your class. You should use your map to illustrate the changes that your chosen empire went through and to give a visual sense of how this fallen empire links to the modern nation/s it would occupy today.

QUESTION 2 HOW DID COLUMBUS'S JOURNEY RESHAPE SOUTH AMERICA THROUGH DISEASE?

One of the biggest ways Christopher Columbus and his fellow European travelers changed the landscape of the Americas was through disease. Native Americans had never been exposed to the diseases brought from the European continent, like smallpox, measles, mumps, and chicken pox. It is difficult to know how many Native Americans died as a result of European arrivals, but scholars generally agree that at least half of the population was killed by disease, with some estimates as high as 90 percent. There were also secondary effects that came as a result of this sudden population drop. Fewer people meant that there weren't as many people around to farm the crops, which in turn meant less food.

Some historians believe that the native groups, while vastly more impacted by disease than the Europeans, did have one thing to share with the newcomers: syphilis. Syphilis is a venereal disease that was present in the Americas before the arrival of Europeans and first appeared in Europe in 1493—shortly after

Columbus returned home. Syphilis infected many famous artists, politicians, and even monarchs of Europe. It might even be responsible for the famed infertility of King Henry VIII of England.

PROJECT 2
MEDICAL CHART

The diseases that were shared through sexual contact (like syphilis) or other physical contact (smallpox) were extremely destructive. How do you think individuals reacted to what they were dealing with physically? Create a character who is presenting with symptoms of one of these Columbian Exchange–era diseases. While your character can be fictional (or based on a real person you read about in a primary account), the person's circumstances should be rooted in research. If your individual is a member of the Inca tribe, he or she should become sick from a disease that affected that particular group. The disease should be contracted in a realistic way, e.g., if the person was a soldier, perhaps he was exposed to disease through blood on the battlefield.

- **Create a profile of an individual, either a member of one of the native groups, like the Aztec, Inca, or others, or a European explorer. Then write up a two-page modern-day medical report for them, as if you could transport one of these people from the 1400s to a modern doctor's office. Give your person a name that fits the time period, create a family history for that person, and describe his or her daily activities. Think of questions your doctor asks you to get inspired, and be sure to have historical evidence to back up your imagined individual.**

Medicine has come a long way since the 1500s. Now, most people can look up medical information on the internet before stepping foot in a doctor's office.

- In your medical report, make sure to answer the following questions: What are the patient's symptoms? Does he or she have a rash on the skin, a fever, or something else? Is he or she having hallucinations? Why was this person more likely to come down with this disease? Remember, this part should be based on your research.
- Sum up your report by diagnosing your patient. What disease do you think your patient has? Since your patient has time-traveled to the present, what modern medicine could he or she take to protect him or her from the disease? Is there a cure?

CHAPTER TWO

THE ORIGINS OF PIZZA

Columbus knew that China boasted lots of riches and resources, but the only way to get there at the time was to either travel over land on the Silk Road or sail around the southern tip of Africa, neither of which sounded like good options. At the time, riches did not mean just gold and silver. Spices, certain textiles, and exotic plants and animals were also considered to be very valuable. So when he sailed across the Atlantic to get to Asia, Columbus was doing so not for the spirit of adventure but to see what kinds of riches he could find.

What's one great thing to come out of the Columbian Exchange? Pizza!

What he found in the Americas was beyond his wildest dreams. The differences in plants, animals, and people were astounding to him, and he longed to show them to his fellow Europeans. Being the first to transfer all these things between the two continents irrevocably shaped our world. Many of the things you might take for granted about a country or a culture were probably influenced by the Columbian Exchange. For example, the Italians gained access to tomatoes only after Columbus's journey since they didn't exist in Europe before then. That means that there was no tomato sauce, and, therefore, no pizza in Italy until well after 1492.

LOOKING THROUGH HISTORY: THE POTATO FAMINE

What do the Columbian Exchange and the Irish Potato Famine of 1846 have in common? Everything! Potatoes were originally from the Andes, a mountain range in South America, meaning that Europeans did not have them until after Columbus's journey. The root starch grew in rocky soil, could easily withstand cold, and was cheap to grow. These factors led it to eventually become a necessary food source for the poor and lower classes of Europe. The crop became such a staple over the next four hundred years that when a mold (which also came from the Americas sometime in the 1840s) infected the potato crop in Ireland, it caused about one million people to die of starvation. It also kicked off mass emigration—to Scotland, Wales, Australia, and yes, America.

QUESTION 3 WHAT LONG-TERM CHANGES DID THE PLANTS AND CROPS EXCHANGED AFTER COLUMBUS'S JOURNEY CREATE IN EUROPE AND THE AMERICAS?

The foods and cultures we think of as so old—and so traditional—hardly are. In fact, many cultural traditions would not exist if it were not for the Columbian Exchange. Europe was not the only landscape altered by new plant life. New crops were also brought to the Americas. These crops would form not just new vegetation but large-scale institutions that no one could have predicted. Sugarcane, for instance, dramatically changed the Caribbean islands. On his second trip to the Americas, Columbus introduced its growth through the plantation system, a way of growing plants that would trap slaves into labor, and trap slave owners and the entire industry into becoming dependent on slave labor.

PROJECT 3
ECONOMIES GONE GLOBAL

It's clear that the Columbian Exchange brought about huge changes in the world, but how did it affect local economies? Pick an area, and explore how the Columbian Exchange created long-lasting change that we can see even today.

- **Choose an area affected by the Columbian Exchange. It can be in the Americas or Europe, but it should not be an entire continent. If you choose an area in Europe, focus on one country in particular.**

Sugar grew so well in the New World that Europeans took over entire islands just to grow it. In doing so, they took advantage of the local population as well.

- Find one primary source that discusses reactions during the Columbian Exchange to the influx of new plants (use the Digital Public Library of America or another reputable source). Maybe it is a chef in Europe who is excited about the new ingredients, or maybe it is a sailor discovering a new plant.
- Research how the new plant or plants affected your area or country. Did it change how people ate? What they smoked? What clothing they wore?

- Ask questions like, "How did this change the labor force in my country?" For example, if cotton was imported, did your country have to create textile mills to turn the cotton into fabric? How did these textile mills change the labor force and affect peoples' lives?
- How did this plant affect your country's economy at large, both in the moment and later in time? For example, in the beginning potato crops in Ireland helped feed the poorer populations, but later it starved them and forced millions of people to either die or leave the country. This devastated Ireland's economy, not only because there were no workers but because there was nothing to buy and no one to buy it. Find scholarly research to back up your claims.
- Find a clear, evidence-supported change that came from the influx of these new plants into your country that we can see even today, and make a claim as to whether or not you think it was for better or for worse.
- Compile your findings into a presentation, using PowerPoint or another online tool, and present it as an economic portfolio to your class on the health of your country. Utilize graphs, charts, and anything else to help illustrate your points.

QUESTION 4 HOW DID THE UTILIZATION OF CASH CROPS DRIVE SLAVERY ACROSS THE GLOBE?

Plants like sugarcane grew so well in the Caribbean, particularly in places like Cuba, that European colonists had a mind to use the entire area for just that purpose. Sugar could fetch a pretty high price in Europe, so their motivation to cash in was high as well. In places like Cuba, Europeans imported many food items, rather than growing them there since the land was thought to be too valuable to use for any other purpose than planting sugarcane.

But sugarcane required a lot of labor to harvest it. Enslaved people were brought to sugar plantations and forced to work. The Atlantic slave trade, in which Africans were captured and brought via the Middle Passage to both the Americas and Europe and forced to labor as slaves, is a direct result of the Columbian Exchange. Europeans viewed the warm climate and open landscape as a perfect opportunity to make money. This economic motivation led to the destruction of African cultures, the loss of many Africans who died during the difficult journey across the Atlantic, and the enslavement of millions. In fact, historian Patrick Manning estimates that more than ten million slaves were brought to the Americas between the sixteenth and nineteenth centuries.

PROJECT 4

CASH CROPS AND THE MOVEMENT OF SLAVES

Create a presentation that shows how cash crops drove the slave trade and what that meant for the financial picture of the Americas.

- Use *In Motion*: *The African-American Migration* Experience's website, inmotionaame.org, to find the page called "The Transatlantic Slave Trade." This provides an excellent overview of the early beginnings of the slave trade and how it was driven by cash crop plantations in the Caribbean.

History isn't always pretty. It's important to learn about the mistakes made in the past so we can have a better future.

- Write down dates, events, major trends, and the numbers of people involved in the Atlantic slave trade. Where were the majority of enslaved people taken? How did the number of slaves influence the amount of the cash crop that was produced in any given area? Where did the cash crops that were grown eventually end up?
- Create your presentation using the information you have gathered. Include financial data in your presentation, such as how enslaved people influenced the local

economies of these plantations and how the cash crops were exported and sold around the world.

- Include at least three quotes from primary sources, whether from slaves, slave traders, or plantation owners.

QUESTION 5 HOW DID INGREDIENTS FROM THE AMERICAS CONTRIBUTE TO THE FOOD CULTURES OF EURASIA?

Massive shifts in diet occurred all over Europe during the Columbian Exchange—from the potato in Ireland, to curry powder in India, to the tomato in Italy. It must have been an amazing time to be a chef. Ingredients like maize, or corn, blueberries, turkey, pineapple, sweet potato, and manioc (also called cassava) all began to be transported from across the ocean.

Europe is still famous for its food—paella in Spain, pastries in France, and pasta in Italy. What new kinds of recipes were the chefs of Eurasia coming up with at the time? How did the Columbian Exchange forever alter our perception of tradition and food culture? How different are the foods Europeans and Asians ate before the Columbian Exchange from what are considered traditional foods in those places now?

PROJECT 5
CHEF'S CHOICE

Imagine you are a post–Columbian Exchange cook. In a country of your choice (preferably one heavily affected by the Columbian Exchange's breadth of new food options), and with

New ingredients allow chefs to be creative. The chefs of the Columbian Exchange era must have loved having so many new ingredients to work with!

money as no object, how would you incorporate these new foods into a traditional pre-Columbian dish?

- Do an online search for "Medieval and Renaissance Food: Sources, Recipes and Articles," which is full of primary source recipes.
- Notice the language of the recipes. Often they are stylishly written, using alliteration, rhyme, or other creative writing devices.

- Research ingredients that were introduced to the country you are researching during the Columbian Exchange.
- Create a new recipe, drawing upon one of the "classical" recipes you've read. Rework the recipe in your own words while adding in the new ingredient.
- Include some reactions to the new ingredient from your chef character within the recipe. For example, if you are a French chef making a pastry with blueberry filling for the first time, you could remark on the color of the berry.
- If you are feeling very adventurous, bake your new/old creation and share it with the class.

CHAPTER THREE

HORSES, LLAMAS, AND OXEN, OH MY!

The Columbian Exchange didn't stop at tomatoes and potatoes. The animals that came across the Atlantic also had an enormous impact. While the animals from the western side

This nineteenth-century image shows Native Americans using horses to hunt buffalo. Horses became one of the most important and influential animals to many native tribes in the Americas.

of the world didn't impact Europe and Asia as much, the transfer was nonetheless important. In many ways, we think of certain things as indisputable. For example, the familiar image shown in Western films—Native Americans riding painted horses across the Great Plains—would have occurred only after the Columbian Exchange. The original horses that existed in the Americas died out roughly when the wooly mammoths did. These horses are thought to have become extinct due in part to hunting and disease.

Horses did not actually exist in the Americas for quite a long time. In 1492, European conquerors brought them over and reintroduced them to the Americas. These horses were bought and traded throughout South America and up through Central America. Sometimes they escaped or were captured by Navajo raiders. After only 150 years of reintroduction, wild herds of horses, mostly Spanish Andaluz mustangs, roamed North America. At that point, the southwestern native groups and Plains Indians were reintroduced to the horse. Being the only beast of burden on the continent, native groups quickly adapted. Previously, dogs had been the only domesticated animal in the region. According to oral tradition, the days before the reintroduction of the horse were called the dog days, and dogs were trained to pull a travois, or a sled made out of tipi poles in which belongings were placed so they could be moved. The horse allowed for tribes to have a much easier time transporting both themselves and their possessions. It also allowed them to hunt faster and larger game, like the buffalo, and brought more tribes into contact with each other, creating more opportunity for conflict over hunting grounds. Today, there are roughly fifteen thousand wild horses that roam in Nevada, Wyoming, and Colorado.

LLAMAS VS. HORSES?

For the Incas and other native groups in South America, llamas were the largest beast of burden available to them. Llamas can carry things, but typically only up to 100 pounds (45.4 kilograms). That means that most Incas had to transport their own things. With the arrival of horses and cattle, people could move around and transport items infinitely faster than they had before. Unfortunately, the sheep brought over by the Europeans often carried disease—disease that killed a lot of llamas. The llama is still used today, especially in the Andes. They are nimble on the difficult terrain and thrive where horses don't.

QUESTION 6 HOW DID EARLY AMERICAN FILMS ROMANTICIZE NATIVE AMERICANS AND HORSEMANSHIP? WHAT DID THEY GET RIGHT, AND WHAT DID THEY GET WRONG?

Our modern understanding of historical events is often very different from how they actually occurred. Thanksgiving typically celebrates a peaceful meal shared by Native Americans and early colonists. The history is actually more bloody, brutal, and racist. Looking critically at our modern culture can help us retrace our steps and see these historical moments—and other people and cultures—in a more factual, understanding light.

As Jessica White Plume, a member of the Oglala Lakota Tribe and director of the Agriculture Department and Land Grants at Nueta Hidatsa Sahnish College, states in her paper on the healing properties of horses:

> **According to the origin stories of various tribes, horses originated here in North America and came to us as relatives and as a gift from the Creator, making it a sacred relationship. After migrating around the world and finally returning with the Spanish in the sixteenth century, the horse nation and tribal people together changed the cultural landscape of North America.**

The modern horse (as opposed to the prehistoric one) had a huge influence on Native Americans, especially the Plains Indians of the Comanche, Kiowa, Arapaho, and Cheyenne tribes (among others). And while the horse influenced every aspect of life from hunting and warfare to trading and intertribal relations, it actually changed the lives of only a few generations of people. The widespread diffusion of horses began only after the Pueblo Revolt of 1680 and reached the tribes of the Canadian prairies by the 1770s. That means that horse culture was only truly active and unrestricted until the reservation period of the 1850s—a little under two hundred years. However, many Native Americans see the horse as a symbol of traditional cultures before the European invasion and an important part of modern Native American culture today.

PROJECT 6
MOVIE NIGHT

Using your knowledge of Native American tribes and nations, analyze a traditional Western film for the details that are both historically accurate and those that are not. What echoes of the Columbian Exchange do we still see reflected in modern culture?

- To get a sense of how Native Americans have been portrayed in film, read the June 2015 *Time* magazine

Movies are a great way to examine a larger cultural perspective from a certain time period. Unfortunately, minorities have often been pigeonholed and stereotyped by the film industry.

article "Why I Won't Wear War Paint and Feathers in a Movie Again," or watch Neil Diamond's 2009 documentary *Reel Injun*. You can look for these sources online or at your local library.

- Pick a film. Examples of a good film for this project include *Stagecoach* (1939), *The Plainsman* (1936), and *The Searchers* (1956).
- Watch the movie and take notes. How does your film portray Native Americans? What tribe or nation are they

from? Do the actors' costumes accurately reflect what Native Americans in that time and place would wear? Pay specific attention to the role of horses in the film. How do the Native Americans use horses? Is this accurate for the setting of the film?

- Using a free online program like Adobe Spark, create a slideshow discussing the role of Native Americans in your movie. Include stills from the film and historical photos. Dedicate several slides to text, explaining whether or not the film was accurate. Also discuss how the movement of horses through the Americas in the early 1500s led to a romanticized view of Native Americans and the real ways in which horses became a part of daily life for Native Americans.

QUESTION 7 HOW DID THE COLUMBIAN EXCHANGE CHANGE THE ECONOMICS OF EUROPE?

In Europe, the buzz about the Americas was palpable. Everyone was excited about the prospect of a whole "new" land to go explore. A lot of people saw it as an opportunity to get rich. Joint stock companies, companies in which individuals give a percentage of the cost related to creating a colony or plantation, started to rise. These types of companies also helped to protect the investor. While European countries fought for dominance over markets, they sought to conquer area after area. Major areas in Africa were colonized, as was India, much of the Philippines, and pretty much all of America. All of this economic growth (for the Europeans) kicked off a new economic idea called mercantilism.

When presenting to your classmates, remember to speak slowly and clearly.

Mercantilism states that a country's power is determined by its wealth, which is built through trading. Part of this ideology supported the notion that since colonies, and colonized peoples, existed to support the mother country with their resources, they were less important.

PROJECT 7
CREATING A COMPANY

Joint stock companies and mercantilism were central to bending the New World to the will of the Old World. Many European capitalists wanted to take advantage of everything the land they thought inferior to theirs had to offer. In a group with your classmates, create a company that deals in exploiting natural resources in the Americas.

- Research the natural resources that are available in the Americas, and select a natural resource in a particular area that your company will exploit. What are you going to sell and to whom? Why is this particular natural resource important?
- What area are you working in: South, Central, or North America? Who are the people you are trading with? Are you working with Spanish homesteaders, Navajo tribe leaders, or Incan elites? Know your market.
- Create at least one problem your company will have to face. Maybe there is another company that is also trying to sell the same resource as you, or it is difficult or costly to transport. Or maybe you will need translators because you don't know the local language. What problems does your company face and how will it overcome these problems?
- Your company has seen success, and now you need more investors so you can expand. Present your case to your class in an attempt to persuade members of other companies to join yours instead. Use an economic portfolio-style presentation, including graphs, charts, and at least one primary source to illustrate the success of your company in the Americas.

CHAPTER FOUR

CONQUERORS AND THE CONQUERED

The people impacted by the Columbian Exchange were not only Europeans and Americans. While Asians were affected, particularly in the introduction of new ingredients to their cuisine, three continents were more affected than any other. Europeans almost exclusively reaped the benefits of the exchange. Native Americans lost between 50 and 90 percent of their populations through violence or disease. And Africans were subjected not only to slavery but also wide-scale colonization.

Colonization and enculturation were both ways in which white settlers put their culture over and above that of the conquered peoples. This was a systematic and strategic way of subjugating them. By insisting on converting the subjugated peoples to Christianity, forcing them to learn and speak European languages, and outlawing tokens of cultural importance, the Europeans dominated these peoples both physically and mentally.

Though the Europeans tried to convert them, native peoples had their own beliefs and practices. This image shows Manco Capac, first ruler of the Incas, honoring people by piercing their ears.

QUESTION 8 HOW HAVE COLONIES AND MISSIONS IN AMERICA AND AFRICA SYSTEMATICALLY CHANGED THE CULTURES WITHIN THOSE CONTINENTS?

Missions are an organized effort to spread Christianity, typically to areas and people viewed as "uncivilized" or "savage." A lot of the time, this just meant different from Christians. After the outlawing of slave owning in 1807 and trading in 1834 in the British Empire (this wouldn't come until later in the Americas), Christianizing regions in Africa became far more attractive to the British. Oftentimes, this included forbidding Africans to speak their languages and forcibly converting them to Christianity. After displacing millions of Africans during slavery, African cultures were continuing to be displaced through colonizing and missionary efforts.

PROJECT 8
CHRISTIANITY, COUNTRIES, AND ENCULTURATION

Create a presentation that charts how one region (later turned country) in Africa experienced the Columbian Exchange.

- Pick one country or region. Stick with West African countries, as these experienced the biggest losses to the slave trade. Countries like Gabon, Senegal, and Sierra Leone would make good choices for this project.
- Research three phases of this project. The first phase should create a picture of how life was before 1492 in this country. What was the structure? Was there one dominant empire or lots of smaller tribal units? What languages did

The maps before and after the Columbian Exchange were radically different. People across the globe realized the world was twice as large as they thought!

they speak? How did they practice religion? What foods were staples in their diet?

- The second phase should chronicle how the Atlantic slave trade affected your country or region. Were enslaved people captured from one tribe and sold by another to the Europeans, or did the Europeans capture slaves themselves? How many people were sold into slavery at this point?

- The third phase should encompass both colonization and the spread of Christianity in your region. How have both of these forces worked to change the culture in this region? What languages are now spoken? What religions are practiced? Some of these regions had distinct tattoo cultures. How has that been lost/reclaimed? Use two primary sources, one from an African perspective and one from a European missionary.
- Present your conclusions to your class as a PowerPoint presentation. You can include contemporary and historical photos and information gathered from your research.

QUESTION 9 HOW DID THESE EUROPEAN EMPIRES CHANGE THE LANDSCAPE OF THE COUNTRIES THEY CONTROLLED?

The empires that started in Europe spread all over the globe. The British, Portuguese, French, and Dutch massively expanded their territories around the world. Many countries you would not think of still count as colonies of these old empires, like Bermuda and the Cayman Islands.

Imagine how different the world would be if the major European empires had not emerged, colonized areas, and subjugated massive populations of people across the globe. It is impossible to say exactly how different it would be, but these empires and the spread of colonization can be directly traced to the Columbian Exchange. The age of exploration was spurred on by the success of Columbus and the explorers who came after him.

What would Columbian Exchange era people think of the internet? You can sit in California and talk with someone from Africa, South America, Asia, or even all three at once!

Many of these empires were enormous. At its height, the British Empire was technically in control of more than 458 million people (which was a quarter of the world's population). Americans and Australians speak English because of their initial British rule, and English spans the globe due in part to their colonies. Christianity has also spread the world over, partially because of its spread by Christian missionaries to all parts of the globe. At one point, the British Empire was referred to as "the empire on which the sun never sets" because of its global reach—meaning that the sun was always up in some part of the empire. This is just one example of the many empires that struggled for power during and after the age of exploration.

DID YOU KNOW?

Australia was at one point a British colony. The island continent has a similar history to many other conquered places around the world. The Aboriginal people of Australia, or the first people, arrived there between forty thousand and seventy thousand years ago. The first known European to visit Australia was Willem Janszoon, a Dutch explorer, in 1606. A similar colonization process happened in Australia as elsewhere, with England claiming Australia for itself, even though lots of people already lived there. In fact, Australia was originally used as a giant English jail, with English prisoners sent across the globe for crimes as small as petty theft.

PROJECT 9
MAPPING THE WORLD

Each empire dramatically changed the economies, landscapes, and cultures of the places they colonized. Utilize your skills to trace the effects of colonization on a map.

- Choose a European empire. It can be the British, Portuguese, French, Spanish, or Dutch.
- Use a free online mapping tool such as ZeeMaps to create a map, marking that country as the head of the empire. On your map, include all the colonies and territories of your

region. Use a key for every area and symbol to keep your map tidy.

- Illustrate the reasons your empire wanted to colonize or take over that region. Was it for resources? If so, what resources? Draw trade routes to show where goods were moving to and from.
- Think about the following questions: How was the geography of each conquered area advantageous to the Europeans? Was it next to a waterway they could use for transportation? Did it have lots of fields for grazing cattle?
- Find two quotes from primary sources, one from the perspective of a conqueror and one from the perspective of the conquered.
- Write a two-page paper using the research you have done, including the primary source perspectives. Analyze why Europeans colonized this region and how it affected the native population there.

CHAPTER FIVE

THE GOOD, THE BAD, AND THE UGLY OF THE COLUMBIAN EXCHANGE

To put a simple label on whether or not the Columbian Exchange was good or bad is difficult. There are many good things that have come from it, including more food for more people, longer lifespans, and a better understanding of global

The painting *Pizarro Seizing the Inca of Peru* by John Everett Millais serves as the cover art of ***Guns, Germs, and Steel***, a book by Jared Diamond on the three biggest forces to shape our world.

cultures. Unfortunately, that understanding has come a little too late. Many cultures have been decimated, if not destroyed completely. Native Americans now live on reservations, areas that were designated by the US government for native peoples to live on after they were forced to move from their ancestral lands to accommodate white European settlers. Slavery destroyed the lives of millions of people, and its reverberations are still felt in the Americas, Africa, and elsewhere today. While cross-cultural exchange may have led to a greater understanding of different

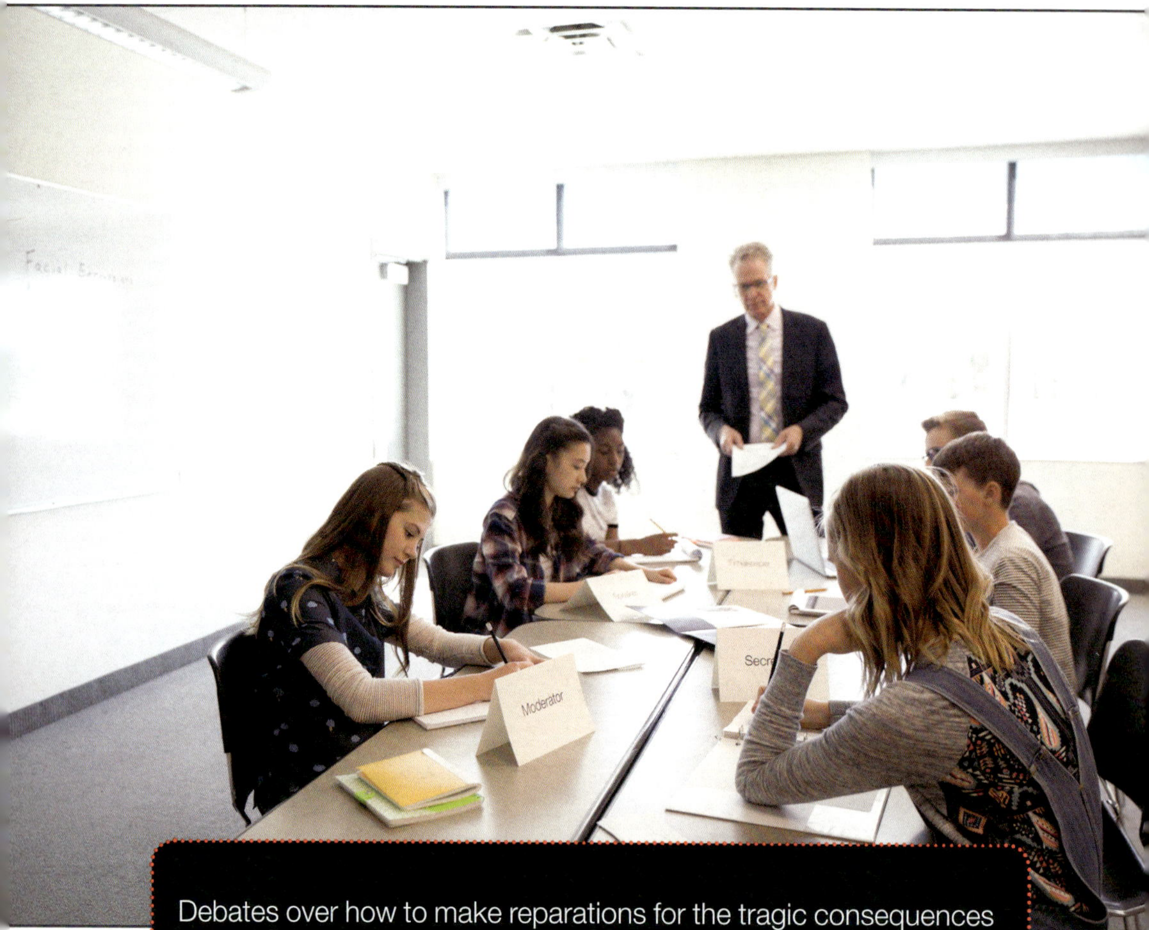

Debates over how to make reparations for the tragic consequences of the Columbian Exchange continue today.

cultures, it also led to colonization. And colonization, in turn, has led to great conflict in the centuries since the Columbian Exchange.

QUESTION 10 HOW SHOULD MODERN SOCIETIES ADDRESS THE NEGATIVE EFFECTS OF THE COLUMBIAN EXCHANGE?

Many people, missionaries included, have tried to heal the wounds inflicted by the Columbian Exchange. People currently called minorities perhaps may not have been minorities if the Columbian Exchange hadn't happened. The echoes from 1492 still affect our world today and will continue to affect us into the future.

To right the wrongs done to indigenous groups around the world, some governments give what are called reparations, which are either payments or some other form of assistance to groups or individuals. People debate whether reparations should be paid to certain groups and for how long. Some people believe reparations are owed, while others think, in some cases, that enough time has passed and reparations are not necessary. For example, Aboriginal people in Australia have long advocated for reparations for the social, economic, and psychological damage they experienced due to European colonization. In 1997, the Australian government began its first official investigation into the forced removal of Aboriginal people and its ongoing effects. This led to paying $73 million in reparations to Aboriginal children who had been forcibly removed from their homes. Many Aboriginal groups have stated that this is a start, although it's not nearly enough.

PROJECT 10
DEBATE REPARATIONS FOR THE COLUMBIAN EXCHANGE

Research the ongoing negative effects of the Columbian Exchange and debate with your classmates on whether reparations should be made to native peoples.

- Find a partner and, together, choose a country whose native population is still facing negative effects that stem from the Columbian Exchange
- Choose a side. One of you will argue for reparations, and the other will argue against reparations.
- Do research on the population you have chosen. What negative effects of the Columbian Exchange did they experience? How are they still experiencing these effects today? How has it led to social and economic disadvantages?
- Do research on the history of reparations. What governments have paid reparations to their native populations? Has it helped these groups or not? If it did, how was it helpful? Did reparations lead to greater equality in the country? Why or why not?
- Write down your argument. Make sure you use facts and statistics to back up your claim.
- Debate your position with your partner. At the end of the debate, look over all of your evidence. Who has the best evidence for his or her argument and why?

QUESTION 11 IN WHAT WAYS DO YOU SEE THE COLUMBIAN EXCHANGE AFFECTING THE WORLD TODAY IN REGARD TO DISEASE, PLANTS, ANIMALS, AND PEOPLE?

Cattle—along with horses—were one of the most important animals brought over on the Columbian Exchange. Coupled with pigs and sheep, these animals became domesticated food sources that were vastly different from what Native Americans, from South to North America, were used to. But as cattle were

This photograph shows a pile of buffalo bones waiting to be shipped and then ground up for fertilizer. Hunting the buffalo to near extinction was devastating to the Plains Indians.

being introduced to the Americas, its buffalo population was dying out, affecting not only native populations but also our food systems today.

After the completion of the Transcontinental Railroad in 1869, "train hunts" were organized across the United States. These hunts were advertised all over the East Coast, for people to board a train, cross the country, and shoot down buffalo from the moving train in droves, leaving their bodies to rot. While these hunts did not begin as an intentional way to wipe out the native population, it came to be understood that that was the byproduct. General Sheridan, the man put in charge by the US government of "dealing" with the native peoples of the West, stated that the civilian buffalo hunters "ha[d] done more in the last two years, and will do more in the next year, to settle the vexed Indian question." By the end of the nineteenth century, there were only three hundred wild buffalo left. Not only did these hunts decimate the buffalo population, but they also cut into native people's food source. Today, we can see how destructive this was, not just to people but to animals as well. The cattle that cover the West are one of the biggest contributors to methane, a greenhouse gas, in the world. Factory farms are a nightmare, and most of the corn we grow is used in feed for cattle, which they cannot properly digest. How hasn't the Columbian Exchange affected us?

The Columbian Exchange had an indisputable, global effect that is still evident today. The changes in population alone were staggering, nearly doubling the European and Asian populations while simultaneously destroying the populations of the Americas. The populations of Africa, while not massively reduced, were forcibly moved around the world, setting off racial tensions that we still see evidence of today. The diseases that proliferated as a result of the exchange altered not only the human landscape but also those of the plants and animals around us. Food was forever different, and food culture has never been the same since. It is important to remember how different our world is from the one before 1492 and how enduring the changes of the Columbian Exchange have been.

PROJECT 11
MODERN ISSUES, OLD PROBLEMS

Identify a modern issue that has roots stemming from the Columbian Exchange. It can involve human rights or other issues involving people, problems with food systems, diseases in animals, or economic problems. Trace your issue back through history to see its roots in the Columbian Exchange. For example, the cattle that have replaced the buffalo have led to problems across the American West, not just in the environment but in our food system as well, like factory farming. There are many different modern problems with roots extending all the way back to the Columbian Exchange.

- **Identify the issue. Find modern newspaper articles that highlight this issue, and discuss its relevance to modern life.**
- **Find four other instances, between modern times and Columbus's initial voyage in 1492, where you see this issue or problem crop up in history. Use primary sources where you can.**
- **Think about how this modern issue might be tied to the Columbian Exchange. Did it stem from racist beliefs and the institution of slavery? Did it have roots in inequality**

Examining an issue today, and tracing it through history, can help us come up with better solutions for the future.

and colonialism? Try to think about how your issue has evolved over time.

- Compile all your information into a PowerPoint presentation. Use images and even audio or video clips to make your presentation interesting. Make sure you trace back your issue to the Columbian Exchange and show how issues do not simply go away over time but mutate and change.
- Take questions from the class. Do they agree with your assessment? Why or why not? Are there any other contributors to the issue you highlighted that you might not have thought of? Take your classmates' ideas into consideration, while using your evidence to back up your claims.

GLOSSARY

ABORIGINAL PEOPLE The native people of certain countries, including Australia and Canada.

ATLANTIC SLAVE TRADE The trade of captured Africans within the Americas and into Europe, resulting in the mass enslavement of African people.

CASH CROP A crop grown on a large scale, typically for luxury purposes. Coffee, sugar, tobacco, and cotton are all cash crops.

CIVIL WAR A war between the people of one area, civilization, region, or country.

COLUMBIAN EXCHANGE The trade of plants, animals, people, disease, and ideas across the Atlantic that began after Christopher Columbus's initial journey in 1492. This exchange permanently altered our world by enhancing and destroying cultures.

CONQUISTADOR A Spanish conqueror of the sixteenth century.

JOINT STOCK COMPANIES Companies in which individuals give a percentage of the cost related to creating a colony or plantation. These types of companies also helped to protect the investor.

MANIOC Also called cassava, this starchy root vegetable has a very high caloric index. It originated in the Americas but is now a staple is most African countries.

MERCANTILISM An economic system in which a country's power is determined by its wealth, which is established through trading.

MIDDLE PASSAGE The part of the triangular-shaped trade in which Africans were captured, forced onto ships, and brutally transported to the New World as part of the Atlantic slave trade.

MISSION An organized effort to spread Christianity, typically to areas wrongly viewed as "uncivilized" or "savage."

PLANTATION SYSTEM A farm of sorts that specializes in cash crop cultivation, like sugarcane, coffee, and tobacco. These systems historically used slave labor.

RESERVATION An area designated by the US government for Native Americans in order to move them off their ancestral lands to accommodate white, European settlers.

SILK ROAD An ancient trade network that spanned from China to the Mediterranean Sea. It was long believed to be the only route across Europe and Asia.

TEXTILE A type of cloth or fabric.

TRAVOIS A sled used by Native Americans made out of tipi poles in which belongings were placed so they could be moved. Before the arrival of horses, they were pulled by dogs.

FOR MORE INFORMATION

Assembly of First Nations (AFN)
55 Metcalfe Street, Suite 1600
Ottawa, ON K1P6L5
Canada
(613) 241-6789
Website: http://www.afn.ca
Facebook: @AssemblyofFirstNations
Twitter: @AFN_Updates
The Assembly of First Nations is a Canadian organization dedicated to First Nation citizens. It provides advocacy campaigns, offers legal and political analysis, and organizes discussion between First Nation citizens and the Canadian government.

Congress of Aboriginal Peoples (CAP)
867 St. Laurent Boulevard
Ottawa, ON K1K2B1
Canada
(631) 747-6022
Website: http://www.abo-people.org
Email: reception@abo-peoples.org
Facebook: @CongressofAboriginalPeoples
Twitter: @CAPchief
The Congress of Aboriginal Peoples is one of five organizations for First Nations citizens recognized by the Canadian government. It serves as a national voice for Aboriginal people in Canada.

Library of Congress (LOC)
101 Independence Avenue SE
Washington, DC 20540
(202) 707-5000
Website: https://www.loc.gov
Facebook: @LibraryofCongress
Instagram and Twitter: @LibraryCongress
The Library of Congress is the research arm of the US government and has the largest library in the world, including many historical documents and photographs.

National Archives and Records Administration (NARA)
8601 Adelphi Road
College Park, MD 20740
(866) 272-6272
Website: https://www.archives.gov
Facebook: @USNationalArchives
Instagram and Twitter: @USNatArchives
The National Archives and Records Administration is the federal government's record keeper. The organization preserves important government records, including those related to native populations. Many of these records are available through its website.

National Congress of American Indians (NCAI)
Embassy of Tribal Nations
1516 P Street NW
Washington, DC 20005
(202) 466-7767
Website: http://www.ncai.org
Facebook and Twitter: @NCAI1944

Founded in 1944 in response to forced assimilation and removal of American Indians, the National Congress of American Indians works to protect the rights of indigenous peoples across the United States.

OurDocuments
Website: https://www.ourdocuments.gov
Email: info@nationalhistoryday.org
OurDocuments is a partnership between the National Archives and National History Day, among other organizations. It provides primary source documents (not just the text, but also high-quality photographs of the actual documents) that pertain to American history.

Project Gutenberg Literary Archive Foundation (PGLAF)
809 North 1500 West
Salt Lake City, UT 84116
Website: http://www.gutenberg.org
Email: help2018@pglaf.org
Facebook: @ProjectGutenberg
Twitter: @gutenberg_org
Project Gutenberg is a volunteer organization that digitizes and archives historical documents. Its collection includes more than fifty thousand items, most of which are full-text public domain books.

Public Domain Review
Website: https://publicdomainreview.org
Facebook: @PublicDomainReview
Instagram: @publicdomainrev
Twitter: @PublicDomainRev

This nonprofit organization and online collection preserves historical public domain documents. Their collection features images from the Codex Mendoza, a compilation of the Aztec history of succession and other details, commissioned for Charles V, the Holy Roman Emperor and King of Spain.

Smithsonian Institution (SI)
PO Box 37012
SI Building, Room 153, MRC 010
Washington, DC 20013
(202) 633-1000
Website: http://si.edu
Email: info@si.edu
Facebook, Instagram, and Twitter: @Smithsonian

The Smithsonian Institution is the world's largest research and education complex. It includes nineteen world-class museums, galleries, gardens, and even a zoo. The Smithsonian Institution offers many exhibitions and resources about native populations.

FOR FURTHER READING

Alexie, Sherman, and Yuyi Morales. *Thunder Boy Jr*. New York, NY: Little, Brown and Company, 2016.

Connelly, Jack. *Christopher Columbus: Discovering the Americas*. New York, NY: Cavendish Square, 2015.

Gunderson, Jessica. *Christopher Columbus: New World Explorer or Fortune Hunter?* North Mankato, MN: Capstone Press, 2014.

Hill, Christina. *Discovery and Conquest of the Americas.* Huntington Beach, CA: Teacher Created Materials, 2017.

Irving, Washington. *The Life and Voyages of Christopher Columbus*. Lanham, MD: Start Classics, 2015.

Kallen, Stuart A. *A Journey with Christopher Columbus*. Minneapolis, MN: Lerner Publications, 2018.

Kavin, Kim, and Beth Hetland. *Native Americans: Discover the History and Cultures of the First Americans with 15 Projects*. New York, NY: Nomad Press, 2014.

McAneney, Caitie. *The Life of Sacagawea*. New York, NY: Rosen Publishing, 2017.

Ponto, Joanna. *Columbus Day*. New York, NY: Enslow Publishing, 2017.

Toth, Henrietta. *Juan Ponce de Leon: First Explorer of Florida and First Governor of Puerto Rico*. New York, NY: Rosen Publishing, 2017.

Wolny, Philip. *Native American Treatment and Resistance*. New York, NY: Britannica Educational Publishers, 2018.

BIBLIOGRAPHY

BBC. "Leif Erikson." Accessed January 23, 2018. http://www.bbc.co.uk/history/historic_figures/erikson_leif.shtml.

BBC. "19th Century White Missionaries." The Story of Africa: Christianity. Accessed January 30, 2018. http://www.bbc.co.uk/worldservice/africa/features/storyofafrica/8chapter4.shtml.

Donnelly, Jim. "British History in Depth: The Irish Famine." BBC, February 17, 2011. http://www.bbc.co.uk/history/british/victorians/famine_01.shtml.

History.com. "Pizarro Massacres 5,000 Incans and Takes Incan Emperor Hostage." Accessed January 26, 2018. http://www.history.co.uk/this-day-in-history/16-november/pizarro-massacres-5000-incans-and-takes-incan-emperor-hostage.

King, Gilbert. "Where the Buffalo No Longer Roamed." *Smithsonian*, July 17, 2012. https://www.smithsonianmag.com/history/where-the-buffalo-no-longer-roamed-3067904.

Lynnerup, N. "Endperiod Demographics of the Greenland Norse." *Journal of the North Atlantic*, no. 7, p. 18–24. 2014.

Malone, Cory, Sarah Gray, Sean Ross, and Katie Ryan. "The Columbian Exchange." Gettysburg College. Accessed January 30, 2018. http://public.gettysburg.edu/~tshannon/hist106web/site19.

Maranzani, Barbara. "After 168 Years, Potato Famine Mystery Solved." History.com, May 21, 2013. https://www.history.com/news/after-168-years-potato-famine-mystery-solved.

Plume, Jessica White. "Four Legged Healers: Horse Culture as Medicine." Tribal College. *Journal of American Indian Higher Education*, May 1, 2016.

Reitz, Elizabeth J. "The Spanish Colonial Experience and Domestic Animals." *Historical Archaeology* 26, no. 1, pp. 84–91, 1992.

Singer, Ben. "A Brief History of the Horse in America." *Smithsonian*, August 19, 2014. https://www.smithsonianmag.com/smart-news/brief-history-americas-complicated-relationship-horses-180960493.

Vago, Mike. "Meet the Norse Sailors Who Reached America 500 Years Before Columbus." AUX: AV Club, November 10, 2014. https://aux.avclub.com/meet-the-norse-sailors-who-reached-america-500-years-be-1798273869.

Weiner, Eric. "Coming to America: Who Was First?" NPR, October 8, 2007. https://www.npr.org/templates/story/story.php?storyId=15040888.

Wishart, David J. "Horse." Encyclopedia of the Great Plains. University of Nebraska-Lincoln, 2011. http://plainshumanities.unl.edu/encyclopedia/doc/egp.na.038.

INDEX

A

Aboriginal people of Australia, 41, 45
Africa, 8, 17, 22, 32, 35, 37, 39, 44, 48
animals
  brought to the Americas by Columbus, 27–28, 47
  brought to Europe by Columbus, 10, 18, 47
  destruction of, 48–49
  domesticated, 28
  trading, 8
  valuable, 17
Asia, 8, 10, 17, 24, 27–28, 35, 48
Atahuallpa, 11, 12
Atlantic slave trade, 22, 34, 38

B

British Empire, 37, 39, 40–41
buffalo, 28, 47–48, 49

C

Caribbean, 19, 21, 22
cash crops, 21
  and slavery, 22–24
cattle, 29, 42, 47–48, 49
Central America, 12, 28
China, 9, 17
Christianity, 6, 35, 37–41, 39, 40
civil war, Incan empire, 11
colonization, 33, 40, 41–42, 44–45, 49, 51
  of Africa, 32, 35, 37, 39
  of the Americas, 10
  of Australia, 41, 45
Columbian Exchange
  food and, 24–25, 26, 27
  disease and, 15
  influence of, 18, 19, 20, 22, 24, 30, 32, 35, 37, 39, 43, 45, 47, 48, 49, 51
  negative effects of, 46
  perspective on, 11
  start of, 8
Columbus, Christopher, 6, 8, 9, 10, 14–15, 17, 18, 19, 39, 49
  influence of, 10, 18
  voyages of, 6, 8, 9, 10, 17
Columbus Day, 8
conquistador, 11
crops, 14, 18, 19, 21, 49

D

diet, 24, 38

diseases, 8, 11, 14–15, 16, 28, 29, 35, 47, 48–49

E

economies, 11, 19–22, 34, 41, 45
  European, 32
enculturation, 35, 37–41
Erikson, Leif, 6
exit projects, 8

F

factory farms, 48, 49
Ferdinand, King, 9

G

gold, 11, 17

H

horses, 10, 27, 28, 29–30, 32–34, 47
  llamas vs., 29
Huayna Capac, 11

I

Incan Empire, 11, 12, 15, 29, 34
Incas, 11, 12, 15, 29, 34
India, 10, 24, 32
Internet History Sourcebooks Project, 12
Ireland, 18, 21, 24
Isabella, Queen, 9
Italy, 6, 8, 24

J

joint stock companies, 32, 33

L

llamas, 29

M

manioc, 24
mercantilism, 32, 33
Middle Passage, 22
missionaries, 39, 40, 45
missions, 37

N

Native Americans, 6, 14, 28, 30–31, 32, 35, 44, 47
  decimation of, 8, 35, 44
  horses and, 30
  romanticizing of, 29
natural resources, 34

O

oral stories, 11

P

Pizarro, Francisco, 11
plantation system, 19
plants, 8, 17, 18, 19, 20, 21,

22, 47, 48–49
potatoes, 18, 21, 24, 27
primary sources, 8, 20, 24, 34, 39, 42, 49
  recipes, 25
project-based learning, 8

R

religions, 13, 38, 39
reparations, 45, 46
reservations, 30, 44

S

Silk Road, 17
silver, 11, 17
slavery, 19, 21, 22, 35, 37, 38, 44, 49
  and cash crops, 22–24
  outlawing of, 37
smallpox, 11, 14, 15
South America, 10, 14, 18, 28, 29
Spain, 9–10, 24
spices, 17
sugar, 21–22
sugarcane, 19, 21–22
syphilis, 14–15

T

textiles, 17
  mills, 21
Thanksgiving, 29
tomatoes, 18, 24, 27
Transcontinental Railroad, 48
travois, 28

W

Western films, 28, 30

ABOUT THE AUTHOR

Alana Benson is an author, researcher, and consultant. She has worked extensively with middle school and high school students both in school and in after-school programs. With a dual bachelor's degree in English and classical civilizations from the University of Vermont, Benson is passionate about both reading and history. She has published several titles with Rosen Publishing, including two health-related titles and another on world history. She is also the author of two books with LexisNexis on identity theft and fraud.

PHOTO CREDITS

Cover Everett Historical/Shutterstock.com; cover banner and interior pages (compass) Theera Disayarat/Shutterstock.com; pp. 7, 43, 47 Universal History Archive/Universal Images Group /Getty Images; p. 9 GraphicaArtis/Archive Photos/Getty Images; pp. 13, 25, 33 Westend61/Getty Images; p. 16 Tuan Tran /Moment/Getty Images; p. 17 Tetra Images/Getty Images; p. 20 Print Collector/Hulton Archive/Getty Images; pp. 23, 40, 44, 50 Hero Images/Getty Images; p. 27 Library of Congress Prints and Photographs Division; p. 31 Lisa-Blue/E+/Getty Images; p. 36 Heritage Images/Hulton Archives/Getty Images; p. 38 Time Life Pictures/The LIFE Picture Collection/Getty Images.

Design and Layout: Nicole Russo-Duca; Editor and Photo Researcher: Elizabeth Schmermund